MY FIRST BOOK

JAPAN

ALL ABOUT JAPAN FOR KIDS

Copyright 2023 by Globed Children Books

All rights reserved. No part of this book may be reproduced or distributed in any form without prior written permission from the author, with the exception of non-commercial uses permitted by copyright law.

Limited of Liability/Disclaimer of Warranty: The publisher and author make no representations or liabilities with respect to the accuracy and completeness of the contents of this work and specifically disclaim all warranties including without limitations warranties of fitness of particular purpose. No warranty may be created or extended by sales or promotional materials. This work is sold with the understanding that the publisher and author is not engaging in rendering medical, legal or any other professional advice or service. Further, readers should be aware that websites listed in this work may have changed or disappeared between when this work was written and when it is read.

Interior and cover Design: Daniel Day
Editor: Margaret Bam

For My Sons, Daniel, David and Jude

Pagoda, Japan

Japan

Japan is a **country**.

A country is land that is controlled by a **single government**. Countries are also called **nations, states, or nation-states**.

Countries can be **different sizes**. Some countries are big and others are small.

Temple Hallway, Japan

Where Is Japan?

Japan is located in the continent of Asia.

A continent is a massive area of land that is separated from others by water or other natural features.

Japan is situated in East Asia.

Tokyo, Japan

Capital

The capital of Japan is Tokyo.

Tokyo is located on the south-eastern side of Japan's main island Honshu.

Tokyo is the largest city in Japan.

Kiyomizu-dera Temple, Kyoto

Islands

Japan is made up of four main islands.

The islands of Japan are as follows:

Hokkaido, Honshu, Shikoku, and Kyushu.

Japanese women in Kyoto

Population

Japan has population of around **125 million people** making it the 11th most populated country in the world and the 6th most populated country in Asia.

Tokyo is the most populous city in Japan, with a population of over 13 million people. Over 90% of Japan's population live in the cities.

Size

Japan is **377,975 square kilometres** making it the 18th largest country in Asia by area and the 62th largest country in the world.

Japan is surrounded by the Pacific Ocean to the east, the Sea of Japan to the west, the East China Sea to the south, and the Sea of Okhotsk to the north.

Languages

The official language of Japan is Japanese. The Japanese language originated in Japan and is spoken by over 125 million people worldwide making it one of the most spoken languages in the world.

Here are a few Japanese phrases
- **O-negai shimasu** - Please
- **Dōitashimashite** - You're welcome
- **O-genki desu ka** - How are you?
- **Arigatō** - Thank you

Fushimi Inari Shrine, Kyoto, Japan

Attractions

There are lots of interesting places to see in Japan.

Some beautiful places to visit in Japan are

- **Fushimi Inari Taisha**
- **Kiyomizu-dera**
- **Himeji Castle**
- **Shinjuku Gyoen National Garden**
- **Sensō-ji**
- **Kinkaku-ji**

Mount Fuji, Lake Kawaguchiko, Yamanashi

History of Japan

Japan has a long and rich history, dating back to prehistoric times. The earliest known human habitation in Japan dates back to around 30,000 BC. Buddhism was introduced to Japan in 552.

Japan was ruled by a feudal system for many centuries until the Meiji Restoration in 1868, which marked the beginning of Japan's modernization.

Japan has never been colonized by any foreign power, making it unique in Asia.

Sado, Traditional Japanese Tea Ceremony

Customs in Japan

Japan has many fascinating customs and traditions.

- Bowing is a common form of greeting in Japan, and is used to show respect and gratitude. The depth and length of the bow can convey different meanings depending on the situation and the person being greeted.
- The tea ceremony, or chanoyu, is a traditional Japanese art form that involves the preparation and serving of matcha, a powdered green tea.

Shinjuku Station, Shinjuku-ku, Japan

Music of Japan

There are many different music genres in Japan such as J-pop, Traditional Japanese music, City pop, Japanese rock, Enka and Gagaku.

Some notable Japanese musicians include
- Haruomi Hosono
- Nujabes
- Ryuichi Sakamoto
- Hyde
- Yellow Magic Orchestra
- Lisa

Japanese curry rice

Food of Japan

Japan is known for its delicious, flavoursome and diverse food.

The national dish of Japan is **Curry Rice** which is a rice dish served with a curry made of meat, potatoes, carrots, and spring onions.

Sushi

Food of Japan

Japanese cuisine is known for its fresh ingredients and emphasis on presentation.

Some popular dishes in Japan include

- Sushi: A dish made of vinegared rice and topped with various ingredients.
- Ramen: A noodle soup dish with Chinese-style wheat noodles, a meat or fish-based broth, and toppings.
- Tempura: A dish of deep-fried seafood, vegetables, or other ingredients coated in a light batter.

Mount Fuji

Weather in Japan

Japan has a temperate climate with four distinct seasons. The climate varies depending on the region, but in general, summers are hot and humid, while winters are cold and dry.

Japan is also prone to typhoons and earthquakes due to its location on the Pacific Ring of Fire.

The warmest months are **July and August.**

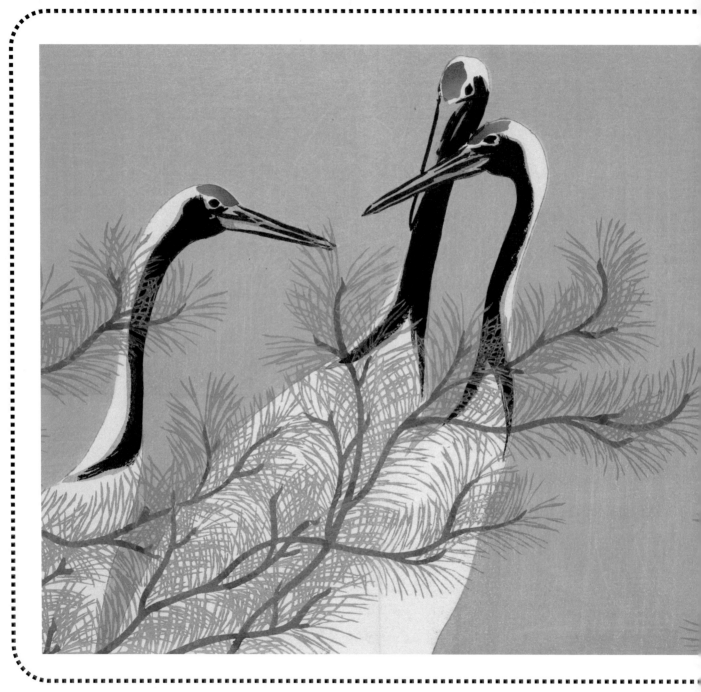

Animals of Japan

There are many wonderful animals in Japan.

Here are some animals that live in Japan

- Snow Monkeys
- Tanuki
- Deer
- Giant Salamander
- Giant Spider Crab
- Serow
- Sea Eagles
- Red-crowned cranes

Itsukushima Shrine, Japan

Shrines

There are many beautiful Shrines in Japan which is one of the reasons why so many people visit this beautiful country every year.

Here are some of Japan's shrines

- Dewasanzan-jinja Shrine
- Kumano shrine
- Itsukushima Shrine
- Kashima Miko Shrine
- Sanko Kumano Shrine

Japanese school children playing sport

Sports of Japan

Sports play an integral part in Japanese culture. The most popular sport is Baseball.

Here are some of famous sportspeople from Japan

- Ichiro Suzuki - Baseball
- Shohei Ohtani - Baseball
- Rui Hachimura - Basketball
- Naomi Osaka - Tennis

Emperor Meiji

Famous

Many successful people hail from Japan.

Here are some notable Japanese figures

- **Yoko Ono – Musician**
- **Hayao Miyazaki – Animator**
- **Haruki Murakami – Writer**
- **Hiroyuki Sanada – Actor**
- **Ken Watanabe – Actor**
- **Emperor Meiji - Emperor**

Bamboo Forest, Kyoto

Something Extra...

As a little something extra, we are going to share some lesser known facts about Japan.

- Japan is known for having the world's oldest monarchy, with an unbroken line of emperors dating back to the 6th century.
- Japan has one of the highest life expectancies in the world, with an average lifespan of over 84 years.
- Japan is home to some of the world's biggest and most successful technology companies, such as Sony, Nintendo, and Panasonic.

Words From the Author

We hope that you enjoyed learning about the wonderful country of Japan.

Japan is a country rich in culture and beauty, with lots of wonderful places to visit and people to meet.

We hope you continue to learn more about this wonderful nation. If you enjoyed this book, consider leaving a review!

With Love

Made in United States
Troutdale, OR
11/08/2024

24585741R00029